CW00762855

Weaving
Scarves and Cowls
on the
10x60 Rectangle Loom

Ashli Couch and Theresa Jewell

STONE MOUNTAIN LOOMS
HOLLEY, NY

Copyright © 2019 by Stoney Meadows Alpacas/Stone Mountain Looms
All Rights Reserved

Illustrations and photographs are by the authors, unless otherwise credited.

All rights reserved. No part of this book may be reproduced or transmitted in any form or by any means, electronic or mechanical, including photocopying, recording, or by any information storage and retrieval system, without the written permission of the Publisher, except where permitted by law.

Published in the United States of America

March 2019

ISBN-13 – 978-0-9998738-4-7

Table of Contents

We dedicate this book

To

Our fellow weavers! Without you none of these books would have been possible. Thank you for your continued support.

Welcome!

We are, as always, super excited to bring you the next installment of patterns on Stone Mountain Looms! I am so very excited about this book because this just happens to be my *favorite* loom! I just can't wait to get you started on this fantastic shape and see all the amazing projects you will create!

Why is this particular loom my favorite? This is my first frame loom to learn on so it carries a special place in my heart but I also have a thing for scarves. Ever since I started making my own scarves on this loom I've fallen in love. I love wearing scarves everywhere now. I wear them all year long; out to work, to dinner, and sometimes just because I can. Playing with different weight yarns has given me the freedom to create winter scarves and summer scarves. And the way continuous strand weaves on this shape loom is just so interesting, I love it.

Now that you know what my favorite shape loom is, what do you suppose Theresa's favor shape is? If I'd have to take a guess, I'd say the square. Why? Well if you've seen her in person you'll always find her working on at least two different squares. She typically has the 3ft square rug loom up and working it as well as a 2ft square. And my gosh, she is super woman on that rug loom! Just give her some rug yarn to play with and soon you'll have a completed rug.

I hope you find your own favorite shape to make projects on. Over the next few chapters, we will walk you through step-by-step instructions on how to set-up, weave, change colors, some troubleshooting and finish your rectangle loom. Once we get through all that boring, but necessary, stuff you'll find a collection of patterns designed by Theresa and myself, for Stone Mountain Looms.

May you weave many beautiful projects and have fun doing it!

-Ashli

Before you get Started

**Always secure your loom to your stand! You never know when it might fall. Securing it can prevent any accidents.
You can tie a piece of yarn around the loom to the stand or we also like using zip ties.

Before you start your project it's always a good idea to know how much yarn you need. If you're not sure, a good rule of thumb is to purchase more than you need of a particular color of yarn so you have the same dye lot. To complete one 10x60 scarf, you need approximately 200 yards of yarn. This gives you a lot of wiggle room for mistakes, and a final border or fringe later.

As always, to start weaving on the 10 x 60 scarf loom you make a slip knot and place it on your corner nail. If you are unsure how to make a slip knot, we have provided a step by step for you on the next page. If you already know how to tie a slip knot, you're ahead of the game and can skip to the next section.

Both Theresa and I are visual learners. Therefore, we will provide as many pictures as we can to help instruct you in starting your loom!
*Pattern 12

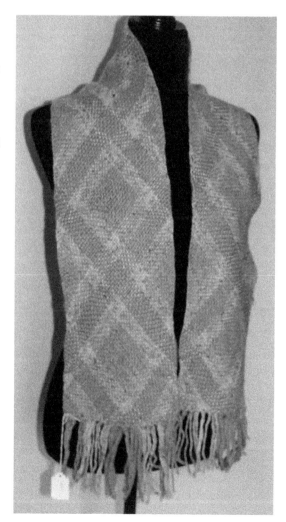

Tying a Slip Knot

A slip knot can be very tricky, but you can do it. We have provided you with an easy step by step guide with pictures to help you with the process.

Step 1: Start by finding the yarn you want to start your project with and find an end. I prefer to work with the 'wrong' end or the end that unravels around the skein of yarn. Other's prefer working with the end that pulls from the center of the skein. Start with whichever end you are comfortable with.

Step 2: Pull enough string out for fringe or enough to make you feel comfortable that is long enough for you to handle. You don't want it super long, just a comfortable amount of string. Approximately 12-16 inches will work nicely.

Step 3: Lay your string on a flat surface. Pick up the yarn closest to the skein and make a loop over near the end of your yarn.

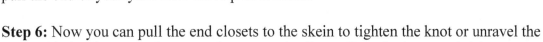

Step 4: Still holding the yarn closet to the skein, go under the loop you just made.

Step 5: Keep holding the yarn and with your other hand pull the end of your yarn until the slip knot forms.

Step 6: Now you can pull the end closets to the skein to tighten the knot or unravel the knot. This is when you place your loop over the first nail on the loom and tighten.

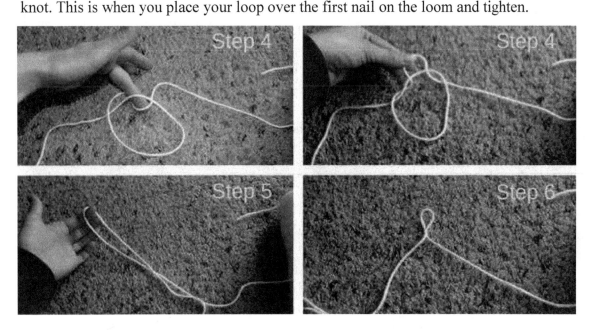

Weaving on your Loom

Feel free to use which ever pattern you'd like to try first to learn. I do recommend having extra yarn on hand, just in case.

Step 1: First get your loom in the right direction. As with all Stone Mountain Looms, the 'markings' always go to the left hand side on the stand. (Unless you're left handed, then you can reverse this and put the marks to the right and start in the top right hand corner). Make a slip knot and slip it over the nail on the top left hand corner of the loom.

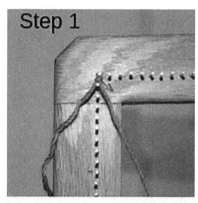

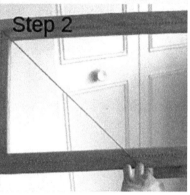

Step 2: Bring your working yarn (the strand attached to the ball of yarn) from your slip knot to the first mark on the bottom of your loom. Continue taking your yarn up to the next mark on the loom. Continue to zig zag to each mark until you reach the top right hand side of the loom.

Step 3: Bring your yarn counter-clockwise around the corner nail. Follow your yarn down and go clockwise around the nail to the right of your first strand. Take your yarn up to go counter-clockwise around the nail to the right of your first strand. Continue this pattern to your slipknot.

*I like to wrap my first strand of yarn around the corner nail and the next nail on the bottom of the loom. This just makes it easier to weave later and will not mess up your nail count. - Ashli

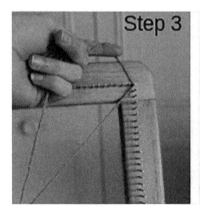

Step 4: Now that you're back on the left hand side of the loom, bring your yarn clockwise under the second nail. Bring the yarn UNDER your first strand with the slipknot to the second nail on the top row.

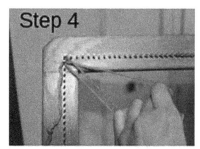

Step 5: Pull some slack on your working yarn. This will get more important the more your weave because it will make pulling the yarn through your work a lot easier later.

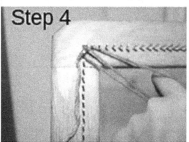

**This is where this shape loom gets a little tricky. Instead of just weaving normal like you would on a different shape loom, the rectangle requires you 'twist' your yarn as you work. I will explain this, with pictures, as we go.

Step 6: Time for your first twist. Grab your magic wand (afghan crochet hook) weave under, over and hook your yarn attached to the last nail you placed it over. Carefully pull the yarn through your work, sliding your working yarn up so the 'loose' yarn, not attached to a nail, goes over top of your yarn attached to the last nail.

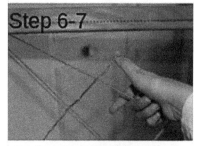

Step 7: Take the yarn attached to the last nail, make sure you have your weave, and place the yarn counter-clockwise around the next available nail to the left of your work on the bottom of the loom.

Woot! One twist down! That wasn't so bad? Right? Trust me, with a little practice the twist will become second nature. Once it clicked *for me, I had a lot of fun with the twist. Are you ready for the next twist?*

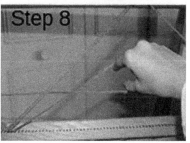

Step 8: Now we are going to bring the yarn up to the next zig zag on the loom. I find this twist is easier to do before I pull my yarn through my work. Working from the left side of your work, go under, over. Bring your loose, not attached to any nail yarn and bring it over top of your yarn attached to the last nail. Hook the yarn attached to the nail on your magic wand and slide through your work. Hook your yarn attached to the last nail clockwise over the next available nail to the left of the zig zag.

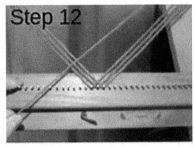

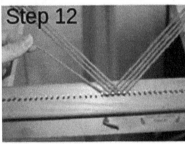

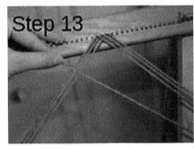

That's it. Those are the two 'twists' you have to master to weave on the rectangle loom. An easy way to check to make sure you did your twist correct is to put a finger under each zig zag 'V'. If all the yarn is over, under you're doing the twist correct. If you see two over's or two under's you've twisted wrong. This can be fixed by working backwards, pulling out your work, until you reach your mistake.

Step 9: Repeat steps 7-8.

Step 10: Repeat step 7.

Step 11: This is where your loom gets easy. Have you been wondering what we are going to do with that loose yarn traveling across your loom? We are going to take care of that right now. It's time to 'place' your yarn since you've already woven it. Bring your yarn connected to the last nail and bring it up to the left hand corner. Go counter-clockwise over the next available nail.

Step 12: After you've placed your yarn on the left side of the loom, you'll notice the yarn is already woven. Grabbing the yarn on the right side of the first zig zag, slide it into place and wrap the yarn counter-clockwise around the next available nail to the left.

Step 13: Follow your yarn down to the next zig zag. Don't forget your weave. Bring the weave down into place, grab the yarn on the left side of the weave, wrap it clockwise around the next available nail to the left of your work.

Step 14: Repeat steps 12-13 until you reach the left side of the loom.

Step 15: Now you're ready to weave again. Repeat steps 4-14 until you're loom is full and you have one more nail left on the left side of the loom.

Step 16: Pulling two strand of yarn through your work is very difficult at this point and you only have one more strand to weave, so instead of struggling with two strands we recommend you 'measure' your last strand. (See picture) By measure, bring your yarn without weaving, over your work to the last nails in your zig zag pattern until you reach the right hand side. Leave enough room for fringe and cut your yarn. Now weave this last strand through your work. Since there is only one strand you do not have to worry about any twist.

> *Weaving the last string can be hard to do depending on your tension. That's why we like to cut our last piece of yarn before we weave it up through the center. Bringing one string up is a lot easier to do than two.

Step 17: Tie off your last strand. Pull your slip knot off the first nail on the left side of your loom and tie off. You can add fringe to your work, or you can simply pull your work off the loom.

*There is no need to 'bind-off' your loom. Your edges are all interwoven and will not unweave when you remove your work from the loom.

Congratulations! You're done!

*I hope these instructions were easy to follow and did not overwhelm you. As I've mentioned before, this is my favorite shape because the twist makes it a lot of fun to weave. And, I love love love scarves. I'm a little bias here. I hope you had fun!

~Ashli

Weaving when your crochet hook is too 'short'

At some point, it will become difficult to weave your crochet hook all the way through your work. This is when you start weaving a few strands at a time, starting from the right hand side. This is hard to explain with words, here are a few pictures and steps to help you.

*Please note that the pictures were taken on a Triangle loom, but it works the same way on the square.

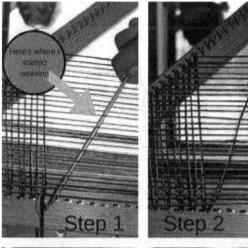

Step 1: Weave part way through your weaving. *Be sure you are doing the opposite of what you did last to keep the over, under pattern.

Step 2: Pull your working yarn through the part you wove through.

Step 3: Keep weaving part of your work, always pulling your working yarn through your work until you reach the right hand side.

Step 4: Pull your working yarn all the way to the right hand side of your work and hook on the appropriate nail.

Fixing Common Mistakes

At some point in your weaving life you will find a mistake in your work. Don't worry, mistakes are easy to fix or you can leave the mistake. After all, this is a human made product. Mistakes can make your work unique.

Theresa and I make mistakes too, so don't worry. We can help you fix them! Here are the most common mistakes we come across and how to fix them.

Too Many Over's or Under's in a Row

A lot of the time you will be weaving and all of a sudden you'll realize you have three over's or under's in a row. And your pattern calls for over, under, over. You decide you want to fix it before you continue weaving.

Here's how:

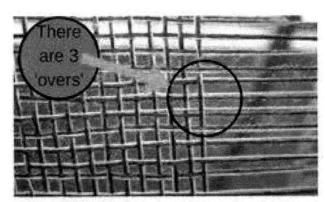

Step 1: Find your mistake.

Step 2: Find your working yarn and work backwards. Slip your working yarn off the last nail you placed it on.

Step 3: Now pull on your working yarn to unweave your work.

Step 4: Keep pulling out your weaving until you reach your mistake.

Step 5: Now it's time to reweave and 'fix' your mistake. Your mistake should be fixed, and now you're ready to continue weaving your project.

Your Yarn Breaks

Sometimes while you're weaving, especially if you are working with 1 ply yarn (roving), your yarn with snap or break. You have several options before you so do not worry.

Your working yarn breaks while you are pulling it through the weaving. You can either pull out your work until you are on the left side of the loom where you can cut the broken piece off and treat it like you're changing colors. Tie the new end to the side, creating fringe and continue weaving.

A horizontal string breaks near the beginning of your work. This is scary and distressing, but we can fix it.

You can keep going as if the string is not broken and finish your work. When you go to fringe, or before you take your work off the loom, you can measure a new string to replace the broken one.

Before you pull the broken string out, here's a neat trick. You can take your new piece of yarn and tie one end to one of the broken ends. Now carefully pull the broken end with your new yarn attached through your weaving. Once you're at the end you can untie the strings, cut your broken string to fringe length and tie the new and old string together.

By attaching the two strings together and pulling them through your work you eliminate the need to re-weave a new string in the old strings place. This goes quicker than if you were to pull the broken string out and using a tapestry needle re-weave the new string in its place.

Changing Color Yarn

Now that you have the weaving basics down you can get adventurous and change color! Is changing color hard?

NO! It's not hard at all!

It's more nerve wrecking because you're cutting your yarn which can be kind of scary. But we are going to walk you through it.

How to Change Color:

Step 1: Get to a place where you'd like to change color, or where the pattern changes color. Make sure you're working yarn is on the left side. The left side is where you will ALWAYS make your changes. This applies to ALL Stone Mountain Looms and our patterns.

     Get your scissors ready. Pull some slack up where your working yarn is over the top nail on the left side. If you're planning to leave fringe pull enough slack for the length of your fringe.

     Cut your working yarn.

Step 2: Don't panic! You did not just ruin your work, I promise. We are now ready to change color. Pick up your new color yarn. Using your crochet hook, weave from the right to the left of the loom, doing the opposite of what you just did on the loom. Make sure you are pulling two strands through at once. Draw the end of your new color up through your work and hook on the next available nail.

Step 3: Return to the right hand side and pull enough of your new yarn through for the length of your fringe. Use the nail you just hooked your new color on as an anchor.

Step 4: Tie your new color with your old working yarn. A simple knot will do. Just make sure it is secure and not going to loosen or slide apart as you pull on your new yarn.

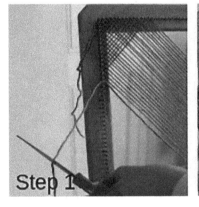
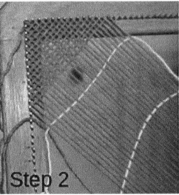
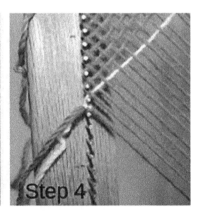

Step 5: Your new color is now attached. Now you once again start weaving.

You've successfully changed colors! You can change colors as often as you'd like throughout your work. Or you can follow our patterns for two or more colors.

Happy weaving!

Adding Edges

You've just finished weaving the entire rectangle, now what? It's time to finish your project and get it off the loom where you can add embellishments like a crocheted border, if you'd like.

We recommend when you get to the last nail on your rectangle, you stop weaving for a minute. Yes, you have one more strand to weave through your work. You can weave two strands up through your work like you have been this whole time or you can, without weaving, bring your working yarn up to the top of your loom.

Leaving enough room for fringe, cut your working yarn.

Now you can weave the final strand up through your work.

When you get to the opposite side, it's time to tie off. You want to tie your last string to the work so it does not unweave.

You also want to tie off your slip knot. I find slipping my slip knot off the first nail before I tie it off easier than trying to pull it off after I've tied it off. You can tie off either before or after you take the slip knot off, it's up to you.

Fringe Border

*I find a latch hook is a lot easier

Now that everything is tied off, it's time to add fringe! *If you don't want to add fringe you can skip ahead to taking your work of your loom.

Both Theresa and I use a knitting needle gauge card to help us measure our fringe (Shown left). Or, if we are in a pinch, we use our cell phones. We simply wrap our yarn around the gauge and cut it, making uniform pieces of yarn.

Using either your crochet hook or a latch hook attach your fringe to your work. We recommend you attach fringe in between every other nail. You can add as much fringe as you like. Pull one side of the fringe through your work and tie with a simple knot.

If you changed color on your work, we recommend you tie the color change ends with the fringe you're adding.

Once you have all the fringe on, you can now take your work off the loom. Just lift your woven edges up and off the nails. Be careful not to snag your yarn as you pull your work off evenly. If you do snag your yarn, it's ok. You can carefully stretch and pull the weave until your snagged piece of yarn slides back into place.

You are finished! Congratulations! You've made something beautiful and you should be proud!

Crochet Border

You've finished your work and have decided to go with a crochet border instead of fringe. Tie off your working ends and carefully pull your work off the loom.

Theresa prefers to crochet borders after her work is off the loom. However, there are others who prefer to crochet their work as they take it off the loom. Do whichever is more comfortable for you.

Once your work is off the loom, find an appropriate size crochet hook and the yarn you'd like to use to make your border. If you've changed colors, we recommend weaving in your color changes before you start your crochet border.

There are so many different beautiful crochet borders available, we recommend you find one you like and follow the crochet instructions available.

Other Borders

Always remember the sky is the limit. There are so many other ways to finish your products, do not feel limited by the two options we have provided.

Stoney Meadows Alpacas and Stone Mountain Looms have a loom available called a flower loom. This loom creates adorable flowers that can be used in your work.

Ashli used the flower loom to embellish the border on this 3ft triangle loom shawl. You can also use the flowers to cover buttons, or shawl pins on your work.

**Always remember the sky is the limit, so get creative and have fun!

Design 1: Regular Scarf

As mentioned before, I am a huge fan of scarves. They go with just about every outfit and can even be used to accessorize an outfit. As a bonus, they keep you comfortably warm. Not only do I enjoy weaving them, I love making regular scarves. They weave up fast and beautiful every time.

When I first started weaving on the rectangle, it took approximately 3 hours to complete one rectangle. Now, I can make one in 1.5 hours! Don't worry, with practice, you'll be weaving that quickly too.

Step 1: Weave the pattern as instructed, or make your own pattern. **You do NOT have to use the same colors as we do in our patterns. You can swap out the colors for different colors.

Step 2: When you're all finished weaving, don't take your work off the loom just yet. You're going to fringe the two short ends. You can fringe your work after it's off the loom, but it is a lot easier to fringe while your yarn is open on the loom.

Step 3: Make sure you're ends are tied off. Pull off the loom and BAM you have a beautiful scarf! Follow care instructions on your yarn label, or hand wash.

Pattern 1 – Sunrise from the Glen

To Complete:

<u>Yarn – Approx Yardage</u>

Gray – 65 yards
Orange/Blue – 80 yards

Nail 1-3 (3 nails): Gray
Nail 4-5 (2 nails): Orange/Blue
Nail 6 (1 nail): Gray
Nail 7-10 (4 nails): Orange/Blue
Nail 11 (1 nail): Gray
Nail 12-13 (2 nails): Orange/Blue
Nail 14-15 (2 nails): Gray

*Repeat pattern backwards. i.e. nail 16=14, 17=13 etc.

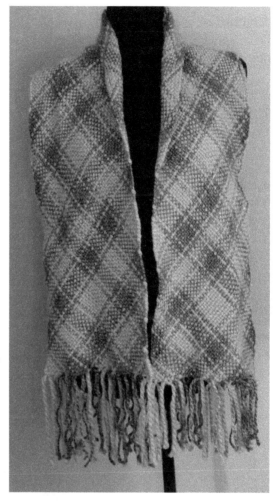

1	2	3	4	5	6	7	8	9	10	11	12	13	14	15

Pattern 2 - Splendid Afternoon

To Complete:

Yarn – Approx yardage

Dark Brown – 90 yards
Light Brown – 40 yards
Tan – 15 yards

Nail 1-5 (5 nails): Dark Brown
Nail 6-7 (2 nails): Light Brown
Nail 8-11 (4 nails): Dark Brown
Nail 12-13 (2 nails): Light Brown
Nail 14-15 (2 nails): Tan

*Repeat pattern backwards. i.e. nail 16=14,
17=13 etc.

| 1 | 2 | 3 | 4 | 5 | 6 | 7 | 8 | 9 | 10 | 11 | 12 | 13 | 14 | 15 |

Pattern 3 - Buttercups on the Dunes

To Complete:

Yarn – Approx yardage

Fawn – 80 yards
Brown – 30 yards
Yellow – 35 yards

Nail 1 -8 (8 nails): Fawn
Nail 9-11 (3 nails): Brown
Nail 18-21 (4 nails): Yellow

*Repeat pattern backwards. i.e. nail 16=14,
17=13 etc.

| 1 | 2 | 3 | 4 | 5 | 6 | 7 | 8 | 9 | 10 | 11 | 12 | 13 | 14 | 15 |

Pattern 4 - Gooseberry Wine

To Complete:

Yarn – Approx Yardage

Gray – 70 yards
Red – 60 yards
White – 15 yards

Nail 1-7 (7 nails): Gray
Nail 8-13 (6 nails): Red
Nail 14-15 (2 nails): White

*Repeat pattern backwards. i.e. nail 16=14,
17=13 etc.

1	2	3	4	5	6	7	8	9	10	11	12	13	14	15

Pattern 5 – Skipping to the Drums

To Complete:

Yarn – Approx Yardage

Fawn – 80 yards
White – 25 yards
Green – 40 yards

Nail 1 -5 (5 nails): Fawn
Nail 6-7 (2 nails): White
Nail 8-11 (4 nails): Green
Nail 12-14 (3 nails): Fawn
Nail 15 (1 nail): White

*Repeat pattern backwards. i.e. nail 16=14,
17=13 etc.

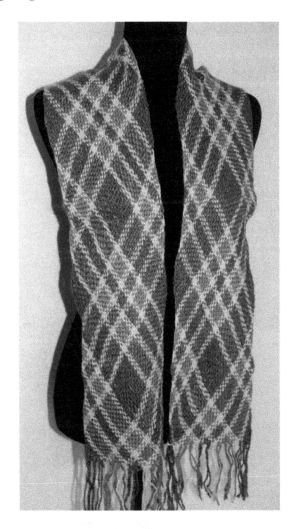

| 1 | 2 | 3 | 4 | 5 | 6 | 7 | 8 | 9 | 10 | 11 | 12 | 13 | 14 | 15 |

Pattern 6 – Another Drop of Ale

To Complete:

Yarn – Approx Yardage

Brown – 60 yards
White – 55 yards
Orange – 30 yards

Nail 1-6 (6 nails): Brown
Nail 7-10 (4 nails): White
Nail 11-13 (3 nails): Orange
Nail 14-15 (2 nails): White

*Repeat pattern backwards. i.e. nail 16=14,
17=13 etc.

1	2	3	4	5	6	7	8	9	10	11	12	13	14	15

Pattern 7 – Wheat and Barley

To Complete:

Yarn – Approx Yardage

Dark Brown – 80 yards
Fawn – 50 yards
White – 15 yards

Nail 1-5 (5 nails): Dark Brown
Nail 6-10 (5 nails): Fawn
Nail 11-13 (3 nails): Dark Brown
Nail 14-15 (2 nails): White

*Repeat pattern backwards. i.e. nail 16=14, 17=13 etc.

1	2	3	4	5	6	7	8	9	10	11	12	13	14	15

Pattern 8 – Steppin' into Town

To Complete:

Yarn – Approx Yardage

Fawn –80 yards
Blue – 60 yards
Gray – 15 yards

Nail 1-6 (6 nails): Fawn
Nail 7-11 (6 nails): Blue
Nail 12-13 (2 nails): Fawn
Nail 14-15 (2 nails): Gray

*Repeat pattern backwards. i.e. nail 16=14, 17=13 etc.

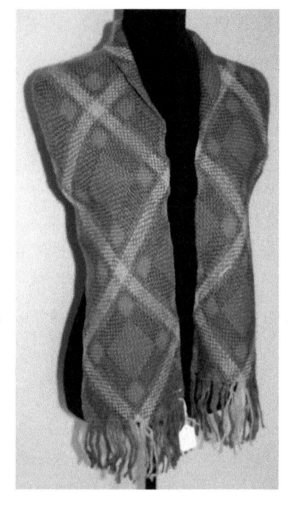

1	2	3	4	5	6	7	8	9	10	11	12	13	14	15

Pattern 9 – Frolic in the Field

To Complete:

Yarn – Approx Yardage

Gray – 60 yards
Black – 30 yards
Green – 55 yards

Nail 1-6 (6 nails): Gray
Nail 7-9 (3 nails): Black
Nail 10-15 (6 nails): Green

*Repeat pattern backwards. i.e. nail 16=14,
17=13 etc.

| 1 | 2 | 3 | 4 | 5 | 6 | 7 | 8 | 9 | 10 | 11 | 12 | 13 | 14 | 15 |

Pattern 10 - Pristine

To Complete:

Yarn – Approx Yardage

Tan – 80 yards
Gray – 40 yards
Green – 25 yards

Nail 1-4 (4 nails): Tan
Nail 5-8 (4 nails): Gray
Nail 9-12 (4 nails): Tan
Nail 13-15 (3 nails): Green

*Repeat pattern backwards. i.e. nail 16=14, 17=13 etc.

1	2	3	4	5	6	7	8	9	10	11	12	13	14	15

Pattern 11 – A Time for Change

To Complete:

Yarn – Approx Yardage

Brown – 110 yards
Variegated Fall Colors – 30 yards
Dark Red – 5 yards

Nail 1-5 (5 nails): Brown
Nail 6-8 (3 nails): Variegated Fall Colors
Nail 9-14 (6 nails): Brown
Nail 15 (1 nail): Dark Red

*Repeat pattern backwards. i.e. nail 16=14, 17=13 etc.

1	2	3	4	5	6	7	8	9	10	11	12	13	14	15

Pattern 12 – Heather on the Moor

To Complete:

Yarn – Approx Yardage

White – 60 yards
Tan – 50 yards
Purple – 35 yards

Nail 1 -6 (6 nails): White
Nail 7-11 (5 nails): Tan
Nail 12-15 (4 nails): Purple

*Repeat pattern backwards. i.e. nail 16=14, 17=13 etc.

1	2	3	4	5	6	7	8	9	10	11	12	13	14	15

Pattern 13 – High Tides

To Complete:

Yarn – Approx Yardage

Brown – 55 yards
Blue –60 yards
White – 30 yards

Nail 1-4 (4 nails): Brown
Nail 5-10 (6 nails): Blue
Nail 11-13 (3 nails): White
Nail 14-15 (2 nails): Brown

*Repeat pattern backwards. i.e. nail 16=14, 17=13 etc.

| 1 | 2 | 3 | 4 | 5 | 6 | 7 | 8 | 9 | 10 | 11 | 12 | 13 | 14 | 15 |

Pattern 14 – Blackberries in June

To Complete:

Yarn – Approx Yardage

White – 50 yards
Red – 60 yards
Black – 35 yards

Nail 1-3 (3 nails): White
Nail 4-5 (2 nails): Red
Nail 6-7 (2 nails): Black
Nail 8-9 (2 nails): Red
Nail 10-11 (2 nails): White
Nail 12-13 (2 nails): Red
Nail 14-15 (2 nails): Black

*Repeat pattern backwards. i.e. nail 16=14, 17=13 etc.

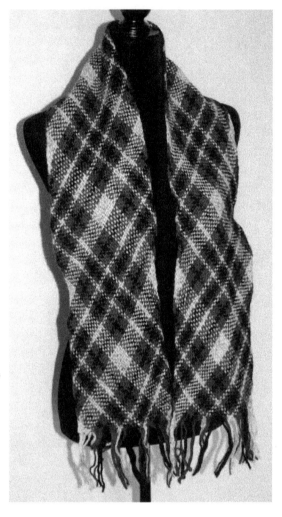

1	2	3	4	5	6	7	8	9	10	11	12	13	14	15

Pattern 15 – A Walk on the Cliff

To Complete:

Yarn – Approx Yardage

Brown – 70 yards
Teal – 50 yards
White – 25 yards

Nail 1-7 (7 nails): Brown
Nail 8-12 (5 nails): Teal
Nail 13-15 (3 nails): White

*Repeat pattern backwards. i.e. nail 16=14,
17=13 etc.

| 1 | 2 | 3 | 4 | 5 | 6 | 7 | 8 | 9 | 10 | 11 | 12 | 13 | 14 | 15 |

Pattern 16 – Tempest Heart

To Complete:

Yarn – Approx Yardage

Red – 60 yards
Light Brown – 30 yards
Dark Brown – 50 yards
Dark Red – 5 yards

Nail 1-6 (6 nails): Red
Nail 7-9 (3 nails): Light Brown
Nail 10-14 (5 nails): Dark Brown
Nail 15 (1 nail): Dark Red

*Repeat pattern backwards. i.e. nail 16=14,
17=13 etc.

| 1 | 2 | 3 | 4 | 5 | 6 | 7 | 8 | 9 | 10 | 11 | 12 | 13 | 14 | 15 |

Pattern 17 – Just Bonnie

To Complete:

Yarn – Approx Yardage

Blue Green – 40 yards
White – 30 yards
Blue – 40 yards
Thick Blue Green – 35 yards

Nail 1-4 (4 nails): Blue Green
Nail 5-7 (3 nails): White
Nail 8-11 (4 nails): Blue
Nail 12-15 (4 nails): Thick Blue Green

*Repeat pattern backwards. i.e. nail 16=14, 17=13 etc.

| 1 | 2 | 3 | 4 | 5 | 6 | 7 | 8 | 9 | 10 | 11 | 12 | 13 | 14 | 15 |

Pattern 18 – Tears of Hope

To Complete:

Yarn – Approx Yardage

Teal – 40 yards
Light Gray – 60 yards
Sparkle Teal – 10 yards
Blue – 10 yards
Dark Gray – 25 yards

Nail 1-3 (3 nails): Teal
Nail 4-6 (3 nails): Light Gray
Nail 7 (1 nail): Sparkle Teal
Nail 8-10 (3 nails): Light Gray
Nail 11 (1 nail): Blue
Nail 12 (1 nail): Teal
Nail 13-15 (3 nails): Dark Gray

*Repeat pattern backwards. i.e. nail 16=14, 17=13 etc.

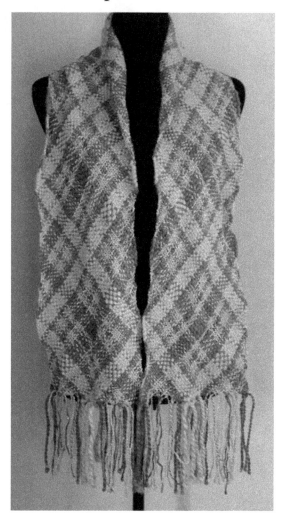

1	2	3	4	5	6	7	8	9	10	11	12	13	14	15

Design 2 – Infinity Scarf

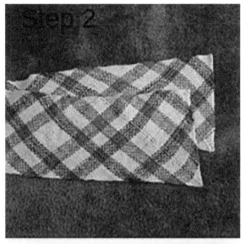

Infinity scarves are just as nice to wear as regular scarves! And you don't have to worry about them slipping off. If you use light weight yarns, these could make beautiful outfit accessories.

Step 1: Weave the pattern as instructed. Tie off your ends before taking your work off your loom. Do NOT Fringe!

Step 2: Weave in all of your strands. This part takes some time, but it'll be worth it in the end.

Step 3: Whip stitch, sew, or crochet the short ends together. You sew them together in a flat circle or you can add a twist before sewing the ends together.

Done

Pattern 19 – Lavender in the Snow

To Complete:

Yarn – Approx
Yardage

White – 85 yards
Purple – 60 yards

Nail 1-6 (6 nails):
White
Nail 7-12 (6 nails):
Purple
Nail 13-15 (3 nails):
White

*Repeat pattern backwards. i.e. nail 16=14, 17=13 etc.

1	2	3	4	5	6	7	8	9	10	11	12	13	14	15

Pattern 20 - Fearless

To Complete:

Yarn – Approx Yardage

Red –75 yards
Variegated Black – 75 yards

Nail 1-15 (15 nails): Red
Nail 16-30 (15 nails): Variegated Black

*There is no repeat in this pattern.

1	2	3	4	5	6	7	8	9	10	11	12	13	14	15	16	17	18	19	20
21	22	23	24	25	26	27	28	29	30										

Pattern 21 - Bringing Roses to Court

To Complete:

Yarn – Approx yardage

White – 90 yards
Brown – 30 yards
Pink – 25 yards

Nail 1-7 (7 nails): White
Nail 8-10 (3 nails): Brown
Nail 11-12 (2 nails): White
Nail 13-15 (3 nails): Pink

*Repeat pattern backwards.
i.e. nail 16=14, 17=13 etc.

1	2	3	4	5	6	7	8	9	10	11	12	13	14	15

Pattern 22 – Pagan Dreams

To Complete:

<u>Yarn – Approx yardage</u>

Light Brown – 70 yards
Dark Brown – 60 yards
Tan – 15 yards

Nail 1-7 (7 nails): Light
Brown
Nail 8-13 (6 nails): Dark
Brown
Nail 14-15 (2 nails): Tan

*Repeat pattern backwards. i.e.
nail 16=14, 17=13 etc.

| 1 | 2 | 3 | 4 | 5 | 6 | 7 | 8 | 9 | 10 | 11 | 12 | 13 | 14 | 15 |

Pattern 23 - Invited to the Keep

To Complete:

<u>Yarn – Approx yardage</u>

Black – 85 yards
Gray – 40 yards
Tan – 20 yards

Nail 1-7 (7 nails): Black
Nail 8-11 (4 nails): Gray
Nail 12-13 (2 nails): Tan
Nail 14-15 (2 nails):
Black

*Repeat pattern
backwards. i.e. nail
16=14, 17=13 etc.

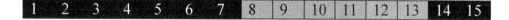

Pattern 24 – Sunshine on my Shoulders

To Complete:

<u>Yarn – Approx yardage</u>

Brown – 90 yards
Yellow – 40 yards
Light Brown – 15 yards

Nail 1-6 (6 nails): Brown
Nail 7-10 (4 nails): Yellow
Nail 11-13 (3 nails): Brown
Nail 14-15 (2 nails): Light
Brown

*Repeat pattern backwards. i.e.
nail 16=14, 17=13 etc.

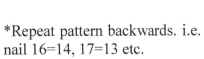

Pattern 25 – A Walk in the Moon Light

To Complete:

Yarn – Approx yardage

Brown – 70 yards
Dark Blue – 50 yards
Variegated Light Blue – 25 yards

Nail 1-7 (7 nails): Brown
Nail 8-12 (5 nails): Dark Blue
Nail 13-15 (3 nails): Variegated
Light Blue

*Repeat pattern backwards. i.e.
nail 16=14, 17=13 etc.

| 1 | 2 | 3 | 4 | 5 | 6 | 7 | 8 | 9 | 10 | 11 | 12 | 13 | 14 | 15 |

Pattern 26 – Storm at Sea

To Complete:

Yarn – Approx yardage

Brown – 100 yards
White – 20 yards
Blue – 25 yards

Nail 1-10 (10 nails): Brown
Nail11-12 (2 nails): White
Nail 13-15 (3 nails): Blue

*Repeat pattern backwards. i.e.
nail 16=14, 17=13 etc.

1	2	3	4	5	6	7	8	9	10	11	12	13	14	15

Pattern 27 - Timeless

To Complete:

Yarn – Approx Yardage

Brown – 75 yards
White – 40 yards
Blue – 30 yards

Nail 1-6 (6 nails): Brown
Nail 7-8 (2 nails): White
Nail 9-11 (3 nails): Blue
Nail 12-13 (2 nails): White
Nail 14-15 (2 nails): Brown

*Repeat pattern backwards.
i.e. nail 16=14, 17=13 etc.

| 1 | 2 | 3 | 4 | 5 | 6 | 7 | 8 | 9 | 10 | 11 | 12 | 13 | 14 | 15 |

Pattern 28 – Blushing Promises

To Complete:

Yarn – Approx Yardage

Variegated Peach – 55 yards
Dark Gray – 40 yards
White – 50 yards

Nail 1-4 (4 nails): Variegated Peach
Nail 5-6 (2 nails): Dark Gray
Nail 7-11 (5 nails): White
Nail 12-13 (2 nails): Dark Gray
Nail 14-15 (2 nails): Variegated Peach

*Repeat pattern backwards. i.e. nail 16=14, 17=13 etc.

| 1 | 2 | 3 | 4 | 5 | 6 | 7 | 8 | 9 | 10 | 11 | 12 | 13 | 14 | 15 |

Design 3: Spiral Cowl

This particular design was created by Theresa. As always, she was playing around with a shape and just happened to sew a scarf in a spiral creating a beautiful cowl scarf! These are great for people who have trouble keeping their scarf in place but want to wear them anyway.

Step 1: Lay scarf flat

Step 2: Create the spiral by wrapping the scarf in almost an "S" shape. *Use picture for reference.

Step 3: Find the middle of your first 'diamond' and line up with the 'diamond' below it.

Step 4: Careful to keep your 'diamonds' lined up, start in the corner of your scarf where the red pen is pointing. Use whip stitch or crochet.

Step 5: Keep whip stitching/crocheting until you reach the other scarf end. Trust me, you will eventually end up at the other side.

Step 6: Tie off your end, cut yarn/string. Now you can either weave in the ends or if they match your fringe, just trim them long enough and leave them as more fringe.

Enjoy!

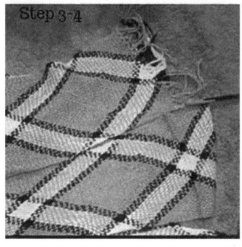

Pattern 29 - Classic Beginnings

To Complete:

Yarn – Approx Yardage

White – 120 yards
Blue – 25 yards

Nail 1-12 (12 nails): White
Nail 13-15 (3 nails): Blue

*Repeat pattern backwards.
i.e. nail 16=14, 17=13 etc.

1	2	3	4	5	6	7	8	9	10	11	12	13	14	15

Pattern 30 – Dazzle Me Blue

To Complete:

Yarn – Approx Yardage

Gray – 55 yards
Variegated Blue – 90 yards

Nail 1-4 (4 nails): Gray
Nail 5-13 (9 nails):
Variegated Blue
Nail 14-15 (2 nails): Gray

*Repeat pattern backwards.
i.e. nail 16=14, 17=13 etc.

1	2	3	4	5	6	7	8	9	10	11	12	13	14	15

Pattern 31 - Traditions

To Complete:

Yarn – Approx Yardage

Black – 70 yards
Red – 60 yards
Oatmeal – 25 yards

Nail 1-4 (4 nails): Black
Nail 5-8 (4 nails): Red
Nail 9-11 (3 nails): Black
Nail 12-13 (2 nails): Red
Nail 14-15 (2 nails):
Oatmeal

*Repeat pattern backwards. i.e. nail 16=14, 17=13 etc.

Pattern 32 - Mossy Meadow

To Complete:

Yarn – Approx Yardage

Tan – 50 yards
Green – 70 yards
Brown – 25 yards

Nail 1-4 (4 nails): Tan
Nail 5-7 (3 nails): Green
Nail 8 (1 nail): Brown
Nail 9-11 (3 nails): Green
Nail 12 (1 nails): Tan
Nail 13 (1 nail): Green
Nail 14-15 (2 nails): Brown

*Repeat pattern backwards. i.e. nail 16=14, 17=13 etc.

1	2	3	4	5	6	7	8	9	10	11	12	13	14	15

Pattern 33 - Goldenrod

To Complete:

Yarn – Approx Yardage

Brown – 100 yards
Green – 30 yards
Gray – 15 yards

Nail 1-5 (5 nails): Brown
Nail 6-8 (3 nails): Green
Nail 9-13 (5 nails): Brown
Nail 14-15 (2 nails): Gray

*Repeat pattern
backwards. i.e. nail 16=14,
17=13 etc.

| 1 | 2 | 3 | 4 | 5 | 6 | 7 | 8 | 9 | 10 | 11 | 12 | 13 | 14 | 15 |

Pattern 34 – Blossoms in the Woods

To Complete:

Yarn – Approx Yardage

Brown – 100 yards
Pink – 40 yards
White –5 yards

Nail 1-6 (6 nails): Brown
Nail 7-10 (4 nails): Pink
Nail 11-14 (4 nails): Brown
Nail 15 (1 nail): White

*Repeat pattern backwards.
i.e. nail 16=14, 17=13 etc.

| 1 | 2 | 3 | 4 | 5 | 6 | 7 | 8 | 9 | 10 | 11 | 12 | 13 | 14 | 15 |

Pattern 35 - Water in the Glen

To Complete:

Yarn – Approx Yardage

Brown – 90 yards
White – 10 yards
Blue – 40 yards
Gray – 5 yards

Nail 1-5 (5 nails): Brown
Nail 6 (1 nail): White
Nail 7-8 (2 nails): Brown
Nail 9-12 (4 nails): Blue
Nail 13-14 (2 nails): Brown
Nail 15 (1 nail): Gray

*Repeat pattern backwards. i.e. nail 16=14, 17=13 etc.

1	2	3	4	5	6	7	8	9	10	11	12	13	14	15

Pattern 36 – Opel Dreams

To Complete:

<u>Yarn – Approx Yardage</u>

Gray – 40 yards
Black – 40 yards
Purple – 30 yards
Dark Gray – 35 yards

Nail 1-4 (4 nails): Gray
Nail 5-6 (2 nails): Black
Nail 7-9 (3 nails): Purple
Nail 10-11 (2 nails): Black
Nail 12-15 (4 nails): Dark
Gray

*Repeat pattern backwards.
i.e. nail 16=14, 17=13 etc.

1	2	3	4	5	6	7	8	9	10	11	12	13	14	15

Reference

Looms and Yardage

*The yardage calculated is only for the loom and a simple border including fringe. Any other more complex border or embellishments will require more yardage. I have rounded my approximate yards up to make sure you have enough to finish your project. Our main goal is you buy enough yarn to complete your project with some left over.

Triangle Looms
6ft Triangle – approx. 600 yards
5ft Triangle – approx. 500 yards
4ft Triangle – approx. 400 yards
3ft Triangle – approx. 300 yards
2ft Triangle – approx. 200 yards
18in Triangle – approx. 150 yards
12in Triangle – approx. 100 yards

Rectangle Looms
21x63in Mobius Rectangle Loom – approx. 500 yards
10x60in Rectangle loom 10x60 – approx. 200 yards

Square Looms
6in x 6in Square – approx. 50 yards
12in x 12in Square – approx. 150 yards
2ft x 2ft Square – approx. 250 yards
3ft x 3ft Rug Square –approx. 600 yards

Diamond Looms
12in x 12in Diamond – approx. 150 yards
2ft x 2ft Diamond – approx. 250 yards

Small Flower Loom
Large Flower Loom

STONEY MEADOWS
alpacas
STONE MOUNTAIN LOOMS
HOLLEY, NY

Meet the Authors

Ashli Couch (Right)

Owner of Bubbles 'n Stitches, her own little crafting business where she makes and sells all-natural lotions along with all her woven and knitted items.

Ashli is self-taught in hand knitting (2011), machine knitting (2018), all natural soaps (2014), lotions (2015), yarn dying (2017), and felting (2017). She learned spinning (2012), frame loom weaving (2012), and peg loom weaving (2017) from Theresa.

Most days you can find Ashli loading up on tea, knitting, weaving, making soap, appeasing her kitties, and working hard on the next weaving book with Theresa.

Theresa Jewell (Left)

Co-Owner of Stone Mountain Looms and Stoney Meadows Alpacas Farm with her husband Chuck Jewell.

Theresa is a self-taught yarn artist and has continued to learn and inspire others. Her knowledge of yarn crafts includes: spinning (2002), yarn dying (2002), frame loom weaving (2003), peg loom weaving (2009), tapestry loom weaving (2017), crochet, and felting.

Most days you can find Theresa at her farm taking care of her 'yarn babies' aka her alpaca and sheep or playing with yarn and coming up with more patterns to share in the next book. She also keeps her husband Chuck on his toes by requesting new shaped looms to add to their ever growing collection.

Meet the Maker
(Well, our LOOM maker)

Chuck Jewell

Co-Owner of Stone Mountain Looms and Stoney Meadows Alpacas Farm with his wife Theresa Jewell. Chuck built all the looms showcased in this book.

Chuck was a professional kick boxer when he met Theresa and became involved with the farm. With no woodworking experience, he and Theresa purchased Stone Mountain Looms, received a crash course in making looms, and the rest is history. Since 2017, Chuck continues to improve his woodworking skills by creating new shaped looms for Theresa and occasionally Ashli.

CPSIA information can be obtained
at www.ICGtesting.com
Printed in the USA
BVHW051213060421
604327BV00008B/396